Cancel the Meetings, Keep the Doughnuts

Also by Richard A. Moran

Never Confuse a Memo with Reality

Beware Those Who Ask for Feedback

Cancel the Meetings, Keep the Doughnuts

· · · · · · · · · · · ·

And Other New Morsels
of Business Wisdom

RICHARD A. MORAN

HarperBusiness
A Division of HarperCollins*Publishers*

HarperCollins books may be purchased for educational, business, or sales promotional use. For information, please write: Special Markets Department, HarperCollins Publishers, Inc., 10 East 53rd Street, New York, NY 10022.

FIRST EDITION

Designed by Caitlin Daniels

Library of Congress Cataloging-in-Publication Data
Moran, Richard A.
    Cancel the meetings, keep the doughnuts : and other new morsels of business wisdom / Richard A. Moran. — 1st ed.
        p.   cm.
    ISBN 0-88730-730-2
    1. Management—Quotations, maxims, etc. 2. Personnel management—Quotations, maxims, etc. 3. Employee morale—Quotations, maxims, etc.   I. Title.
    HD38.M583 1995   94-46396
    658—dc20

95 96 97 98 99 ❖/HC 10 9 8 7 6 5 4 3 2 1

To the children,
Scott, Megan, Brady, and John
May all of them be independent as they prosper,
learn common sense, be intellectually curious,
and always know how to act.

Acknowledgments

A number of people helped compile this book, but the real contributors continue to be those articulate employees at all levels in all types of organizations who are slogging it out day to day in the complex organizations we've built. I hope the people doing real work never stop talking to me—and I hope I never stop listening.

I am indebted to my colleagues at Price Waterhouse for their support and allowances—especially all of the world-class consultants in Organization Change Practice in both San Francisco and New York. And to Bill Dauphinais, a special thanks for continued encouragement and interest.

A surprise and an inspiration have been all those readers who wrote to me with their own pieces of wisdom. Keep them coming.

A special thank-you list of contributors is at the end of the book.

Frank Mount, Lisa Berkowitz, and the rest of the very professional staff at HarperCollins keep me from leaving the laptop at home.

The Big Family deserves thanks for being such fans—John, Louise, Jack, and Tim. And to my closest circle, the Family, real gratitude for being my constant reminder that life doesn't have to be as complex as we tend to make it and that books can be a reminder to simplify. So my special thanks go to Carol and the kids, who make me smile and who are the source of so much material. "We love our bread, we love our butter, but most of all, we love each other."

Introduction

A very harried supervisor in a large company recently told me about the value of common sense in business. He explained, "All this damn company has to do to make things better is fix morale. I've never seen it so bad. Then they need to give us time to return our messages. I'm tired of running around with little pink slips in my pocket, feeling guilty. They also need to tell all those people in corporate to turn off their phone mail and talk to us in person every once in a while. Lastly, they need to bring in jelly doughnuts whenever there's a meeting. That would either kill all the meetings since they won't pay for doughnuts or give us a good reason to attend them."

I couldn't have summarized the essence of what's going on in business today any better than that if I had interviewed a dozen CEOs.

People want to feel better about the place where they work, want to have some sense of control and responsiveness, want to do "real" work and not attend meetings. And they want to feel that they belong.

What I want to convey to people with this, my third book, is a sense of hope that there are ways to enjoy your career, find time for messages as well as other important activities, and, yes, feast on those jelly doughnuts without feeling guilty. How? By following those same three simple principles that are the foundation for all of my books:

Know how to act.

Take control of your career.

Strike a balance between work and the rest of your life.

I try to make all of my books hopeful. Too many people at all levels are losing that most basic of commodities: hope. Hope that "things" will get better. Those "things" can change, but you have to change them. I hope you enjoy the book and feel inspired to change morale, get to those messages, and savor those doughnuts.

Cancel the Meetings, Keep the Doughnuts

1. Remember what it was like when you were waiting to sit at the grown-up table at Thanksgiving. When you deal with the "new kids" in the organization, think of what it was like when you were finally invited to change seats.

2. Life may not be fair in the short term, but it does even out in the long term. Butthead bosses do get theirs in the long term.

3. Give in-laws lottery tickets for their birthdays.

4. When there are tons of sarcastic, cynical cartoons and caricatures in everyone's cubes and offices, there is probably a problem.

5. Before you create an organizational structure based on beliefs, make sure the beliefs are sound and based on customer and employee data.

6.   Always carry a paperback with you when traveling. Never get on an airplane without something to read. If the person next to you has nothing to read, give them something to read.

7.   Learn to listen to clients, customers, and employees and base your actions on what you hear. If people on your team are not good listeners, interpret for them until they become good listeners.

8.   If you don't have time to coach the Little League team, either make the time, get lots and lots of help, or don't volunteer.

9. If you go out to dinner with a group and you don't have cash, don't think people won't notice when you put the entire bill on a credit card that rewards you with frequent flier miles.

10. Fear is not a good motivator. It only works in the short term.

11. Cigarette butts are litter. People who would never throw anything else on the ground believe a butt is not litter. It's not true.

12. Measures that penalize people don't work.

13. Don't be away from home for more than three days at a time.

14. Organization change initiatives always provide the opportunity to go after cost.

15. Technology should allow geography to be no big deal.

16. The creation of any organization is a series of compromises.

17. If one of your colleagues shows up wearing exactly the same thing you're wearing, do something that won't have you next to each other all day.

18. Don't complain about "deadwood." Figure out ways to get rid of it.

19. Allocate more time for any job than you think it will take.

20. Purchasing decisions should be based on what the people who will be using the item(s) need and not just on the cost.

21. Work "without a net." Don't build systems or organizations around something that has never happened—unless you're NASA.

22. Making a decision and doing something is better than doing nothing.

23. Ask for input only if you plan to do something with it and about it.

24. The only thing that's read in most reports is the executive summary. Make sure that section really tells the story.

25. Any effort that simplifies and standardizes processes is good.

26. Whenever everyone agrees that something is a bad idea, it probably is—so don't try to implement it.

27. The word *we* is much more powerful than the word *they*. Too many "theys" make for a victimized organization.

28. Always be able to answer the question for yourself and those who work around you, "Why do I work here?"

29. If the only answer to "Why do I work here?" is "For the money," start putting a transition plan together.

30.   The words *computer conversion* are a signal that work will be done manually for a while.

31. "Good ol' boy" systems should always be replaced by performance-based systems.

32. If Employee of the Month systems work, why is that parking place always empty?

33. Make sure to give *short* speeches after dinners where people have been drinking.

34. Give surprise birthday parties only for those who will appreciate them. Let them know in advance.

35. Guessing between the essential, the critical, and the absolutely necessary is how most people spend their time on the job. The shades of difference could make the difference between success and failure.

36. Most work activities are neither essential, critical, nor absolutely necessary.

37. Most big problems look bigger than they are.

38. Self-directed work teams require lots of direction.

39. Mushroom management—when employees are kept in the dark and fed fertilizer—never works. Employees are very adept at guessing the truth.

40. Find out who is staying in the hotel room next to you before you do anything you wouldn't want them to hear.

41. If, while in your underwear, you lock yourself out of your hotel room, call the front desk and hide beside the ice machine.

42. Service means never having to say you're sorry.

43. Don't blow dust out of your glasses all the time. (What is that stuff anyway?)

44. Don't charge hotel movies to clients.

45. Read your junk mail occasionally. It will tell you who is selling what and where people think there are dollars to be made.

46. Assume that little aluminum ketchup packets will always spill on your clothes.

47. If the shampoo comes in a little aluminum ketchup packet, open it before you hop in the shower and get your hands wet.

48. In your voice mail greeting, tell people how to bypass the greeting so that they may leave you a message more quickly if desired. Why don't companies standardize this by using the one or the pound sign?

49. Never assume people will understand acronyms.

50. Get involved in the management of not-for-profit organizations. You can get experience there that you can no longer get in large organizations.

51. Read a basic personal-finance-and-investment guide such as the *Dun & Bradstreet Guide to Your Investments* or *Money* magazine.

52. Organizations should have one mission that is clearly understood. Everyone may have their own interpretation, but the interpretation should be a variation on the same theme.

53. "What's in it for me?" is the wrong question. A better one is, "Is it in my best interest in the long term to . . . ?"

54. Credibility means people believe you will do it, not people hear what you say.

55. Sending too many messages to your children or employees means they won't know what to do.

56. Abdication of responsibility without a reason will come back to haunt you and probably reduce your job to something less than you want it to be.

57. Put the big vertical metal file cabinets in the common areas, not in your office.

58. When someone describes your company or products as neither low-cost nor differentiated, think about how long you will be working there.

59. Never say no to an offer to relocate without at least considering it.

60. When a consultant from a search firm calls, take the call. You never know what pleasant surprises may be on the other end.

61.   Provide names to search consultants when you can. You may be helping those friends who want a change but don't know it yet.

62.   Off-hand comments will always get you in trouble at work.

63. Don't make light or fun of your organization's core business. You will offend everyone who shows up to perform that work on any given day.

64. Life is not like the movies. People do lose their jobs, get hurt on the job, and have problems dealing with the day-to-day stress. Consider yourself lucky when things are going well and enjoy it.

65. Although we don't know it at the time, where we elect to go to college is one of the most important decisions we will make in our lives. Remember that when people ask you for advice about college.

66. Don't wear T-shirts that say something that would offend your mother. Somebody's mother will see it.

67. When traveling with your boss, make sure you have good directions. If you get lost, you'll get blamed.

68. Know the history of your organization. It will give you some clues about the future.

69. When you go to family reunions, be prepared to easily describe what you do.

70. Worry about intimacy at work. If things seem to be getting a little chummy, they probably are and people will notice.

71. Your diet isn't working until someone asks you if you've been losing weight.

72. Every once in a while, surprise your spouse and meet him or her at the airport. It will be a much appreciated surprise.

73. Take too many photos of your children.

74. Never play a Walkman so loudly that the people around you can hear it.

75. Watch the movie *Father of the Bride* if you have a daughter. It will help you prepare.

76. Send your own photo and promotion announcement to the local newspaper if the company won't do it.

77. Give leaders a chance. Most organizational and policy issues are not solved quickly or without pain. Increments toward a positive end is often the only option.

78. The opposite of gridlock is risk taking. When things are getting stuck, increase your willingness to take risks.

79. Phone mail is like an in-box. Handle each call once and don't let them pile up too high.

80. "Checking out" someone almost always gets noticed—if not by the checkee then by others in the area.

81.   Don't pat short people on the head.

82. Discuss your day when you get home (although not to excess). It will help others understand your work.

83. Worry about intimacy within your family and in relationships. If you believe you're losing it, you probably are.

84. Don't use the word *okay* as a punctuation mark and don't end every sentence with a question mark.

85. Organizations have more filters than they have effective communications vehicles. Know what filters the information has been through by the time you receive it.

86. Leadership is more about communications and credibility than it is about policy and performance.

87. If you ask for feedback, don't expect to hear what you want.

88. Always provide a context to help people understand.

89. Real change and success will happen when you hear: "I like it"; "I'll use it on the job"; "I see a change because of it"; and "There's a dollar return in it."

90. Consider the hassle-to-enjoyment ratio before you do anything like go away for a weekend.

91. Avoid the "Abilene Paradox" where everyone does something that no one wants to do because no one could make up their mind.

92. If you're dating someone in the office, don't expect people to talk to you about it. Do expect them to talk to each other about it, however.

93. Anyone whose job title includes the phrase "decision support" probably slows decisions down.

94. "Centrally located" means far away for everyone, not just a few.

95. If there's no slide on the overhead, turn the machine off.

96. Never eat anything bigger than your head.

97. If there is a Phase One, the project could take years. Plan accordingly.

98. Always double-check your buttons and zippers before you stand up in front of an audience.

99. If you're not sure if the tie or the shoes match, they don't. Wear something else.

100. Automated customer service is often an oxymoron. Make changes if it is.

101. When you set up a "Helpline," you create expectations. Make sure you can live up to them.

102. The more sophisticated the computer or phone system, the more time people spend figuring out the system rather than doing real work.

103. Executives with bathrooms in their offices probably don't spend a whole lot of time with employees.

104. Don't ever sell anything you wouldn't use.

105. Apply the lessons from Dr. Seuss books to your own organization and make policies as simple to understand as his books.

106. In a management shake-up, if no one loses their job, it isn't a shake-up.

107. There are very few places where you can get away with wearing a Hawaiian shirt.

108. Know where you are in the "value chain" and make sure you're providing value.

109. If you raise expectations, performance needs to be raised too.

110. If the water must be shut off to do a repair, you need a plumber. If the electricity must be shut off, you need an electrician.

111. When your boss always uses phrases like "in the crosshairs" or "get a bead on them," look for another boss—unless you're in the army.

112. There are at least two people you should never offend: your boss's assistant and your boss's spouse. Either could make your life miserable.

113. Always create a flurry of activity three months before performance-review time. It will be fresh in your supervisor's mind.

114. Know the image you want to project when you join an organization. Reversing first or undesirable impressions is almost impossible.

115. Never complain about a peer's promotion. You will only look petty and jealous. There will always be someone who gets a better deal than you but your turn will come.

116. Notice what others at your level think they're too good to do and learn it well. You'll get a reputation as someone who gets the job done.

117. Learn to be a sponge. Observe everything and everyone around you. The information will come in handy later.

118. Most companies know how to cut costs because they've had lots of practice.

119. Never leave the men's room with your tie slung over your shoulder or tucked into your belt.

120. The fear of being average is a powerful motivator for ambitious people. Listen to that fear if it's bubbling up.

121. Look behind you before you slam your airline seat into a reclined position. If there's a lap baby or anyone using a laptop computer, keep your seat in the upright position.

122. When jogging, assume all untethered dogs will bite you. Assume all dogs that look or sound mean are not tied up.

123. Create a logic to any decisions you make, at least in your own mind.

124. No matter how many meetings there are to discuss the issue, the final decision is still made in the hallway.

125. If accused of checking your brains at the door, retort with a strong and clear rejoinder.

126. There are very few "standard operating procedures." Those that do exist will soon be changed or eliminated.

127. If your organization talks about replacing your job function with technology, don't look for another job doing the same thing. Learn the technology.

128. Overnight successes don't exist.

129. Microwave popcorn in the office always smells better than it is and will make a mess of your work.

130. Throw away any ties or scarves with any kind of oil stain on them.

131. It's one thing to learn from others and bend their ideas to your needs. It's quite another thing to steal ideas and not give credit.

132. Never tell anyone you like them better than someone else.

133. Once-in-a-lifetime opportunities are never to be missed. If the opportunity interferes with starting a job, take the opportunity and delay the job.

134. Give people space when talking. Gomer Pyle never liked to listen to Sergeant Carter.

135. Job concern is inversely proportional to the level of contribution you know you are making. The less the contribution, the higher the concern.

136. "It's the union" is never an appropriate excuse for management or rank and file.

137. Not utilizing the skills of employees is the worst crime of management.

138. Do not collect or post ding letters when looking for a job. It will only make you feel worse. Instead, frame your offer letter.

139. The administrative staff is not a maid service. Clean up after yourself and don't leave dirty coffee cups in the sink or in the conference room.

140. If you work with a subcontractor, agree on a budget prior to commencing work.

141. If after asking a Magic 8 Ball the response is always "Outlook hazy, try again," get another forecasting mechanism.

142. Never surprise anyone with the size of your invoice.

143. Whenever the scope of a project changes, rates and fees will change also.

144. When you speak with a hushed voice while in your cube, people will assume you're talking to your mother or arranging a job interview.

145. Be known as someone who is able to set a VCR timer and will do so rather than watch 12:00 blink incessantly.

146. Certain parts of our bodies and organizations never die—they have to be killed. Teeth and morale are good examples.

147. Working in self-directed teams means there is no traditional foreman or supervisor. Don't let anyone act that way on your team.

148. When the raise that you receive is not enough, make sure people know your feelings even if there's no chance that the dollars will change. The commotion may help next time.

149. The fastest way to turn the aircraft carrier in the proverbial lagoon is to blow it up and reassemble it facing in the right direction.

150. Remember that lots of other people are reading the same advice that you are about stock picks. Do your own homework as well.

151. Negotiating by using fax machines may save you a lot of emotional energy.

152. Take an internship in the family business only if you never plan to work in the family business.

153. A key element in making a good career decision is the concept of worth. Choose a career from which either you or someone else will derive some worth.

154. Don't chew on a pen before you give it to someone to use.

155. Ignore all bad news about the career field you love and have chosen.

156. When considering long-range career plans, think in terms of short increments that will lead somewhere.

157. Some people do get hired only because they've been so persistent that human resources wants to get rid of them. Persistence does pay.

158. There is an inverse relationship between romance and money. The more romantic a product, the less likely that you will make money from it. The real money may be in toilet seats and car mufflers.

159. One of the highest compliments you can be paid is to be called a Renaissance person.

160. There is no such thing as a new hire probationary period. We're all on probation every day.

161. Guarantees of security should never be believed.

162. Follow your heart as much as you follow the analysis. Don't choose between the two; combine the two.

163. Make sure your glasses are clean. It's hard to listen to someone when there are tear droppings all over the lenses. It's even worse if the glasses are crooked.

164. Even if you are a great performer, if you quit your job and then change your mind and want to go back, don't expect to get rehired or even considered at the same level.

165. Great ideas and solutions to problems often occur right before you fall asleep at night. Get up and write them down or they will be lost in the morning.

166. If you fall asleep in a meeting, assume people will notice, no matter how many people are in attendance.

167. Sloppiness always costs money.

168. Understand basic statistics so you can tell when someone is using them to lie.

169. Lie on your résumé or application only if you want to get fired after you start the job.

170. Never allow your photo to be taken for a company publication while you're holding a drink.

171. The biggest job worry will be the opportunities you missed if you didn't experiment or try to improve things.

172. When choosing a major in college, if you don't enjoy the subject or the classes, you won't like the career.

173. If you feed your small children breakfast, check your cuffs, your elbows, and the seat of your pants for cereal before going to work. Cheerios tend to multiply and follow you.

174. When it rolls downhill, push it back up. When it gets thrown over the wall, throw it back.

175. Perks like company-sponsored day-care and workout facilities are never to be taken for granted. As soon as they are, they'll be taken away.

176. Don't worry if you're making it up as you go along. Most others are too.

177. Pro bono means free. Period.

178. "Deadwood" on the job should never be tolerated. If you know you're deadwood, quit or retire. If you're surrounded by deadwood that no one will address, change jobs.

179. Career skills don't ever get wasted. No matter what the job or how far afield, you will drag components of it with you to the next job.

180. When told you don't understand the big picture, ask to see that big picture.

181. Learn from our friends in Washington: Nothing gets accomplished unless people listen to each other and are willing to make compromises for a common goal.

182. Become familiar with the system at Kinko's and other copy/computer/printer facilities. These places can save your life when faced with a deadline. If you're on a deadline and not familiar with the system, take someone who is.

183. Be creative in sending corporate gifts. Everyone already has the Lucite cubes and Plexiglas quartz clocks. Give away old insulators or fishing reels instead.

184. If you ever say anything like "I'm a _____ (fill in the blank: college graduate, laid-off middle manager, retired military officer . . .) with no future," change your thinking.

185. If you believe you have no future, you don't.

186. If you have changed jobs frequently in a short period of time by either getting fired or quitting, there might be more going on than just meeting the futurists' predictions that we will all have eight careers in our lifetime.

187. Don't accept broad labels like Generation X. They are almost always negative and are created by the media for nothing more than a cover story.

188. Programs created to induce minorities into certain careers are more than lip service.

189. Don't be surprised if job interview questions are like a case study. Expect to hear sentences like "I'm going to describe a situation to you."

190. Never take credit for an idea that is not your own.

191. Nightmares where you go to jail or get hurt will help you appreciate the fact that you're free and healthy. If you feel sorry for yourself, eat an anchovy pizza right before you go to bed.

192. Photos of dogs are not equivalent to photos of children.

193. No one should be interested in your sex life. Don't discuss it at work.

194. Choose role models carefully and understand the costs of his or her success.

195. Diversity initiatives are not methods to meet quotas. They are a means to increase productivity.

196. Don't answer your own questions, especially if they are part of an evaluation. It rarely plays well to say, "Were my expectations met? I don't think so."

197. Time-outs for children always get their attention. Think of the corollary that would apply in your work setting.

198. When going on a business trip, pack the night before and remember that the X-ray machines will show what you have packed.

199. Avoid taking golf clubs on business trips unless the trip is specifically intended for golf.

200. Encourage any venue for good ideas.

201. If you figure out a way to save time, don't read the newspaper. See what else you can do.

202. Don't do anything at any company-sponsored event that you don't want photographed and displayed on the bulletin board on Monday.

203. Dogs that beg are annoying. Don't imitate them.

204. Every job change decision is a big one.

205. Long-shot statements like "The chances of this happening are as good as winning the lottery" sometimes come true. Be careful.

206. Smelling something burning is never a good sign.

207. Smelling popcorn cooking in the office is a sign that it's time to take a break. A group will form somewhere in the hall.

208. Paying fees, even high ones, is worth it if those fees provide a big return, even in peace of mind.

209. Rearrange any meeting room until everyone feels comfortable, even if it means stopping the meeting temporarily.

210. Learn how to really listen to what people are telling you. If you're trying to tell someone something and you can see that they don't "get it," tell them in a different way.

211. When the organizational motto is anything like "All we ever do is rotate bald tires," look for another job.

212. In talks with children it's best to change levels or lower your elevation, even if it means getting on your knees. In talking with people at work, do the same thing.

213. Don't be afraid to show some emotion and conviction. Shake hands with people like you mean it.

214. Watch the movie *Planes, Trains, and Automobiles* before you choose a career in consulting.

215. Employees will continue to be asked to do more with the same resources—or with even less. Get used to it.

216. For better or worse, the great-paying blue-collar jobs are disappearing. Do anything you can to get through college.

217. The only college textbooks you should not throw away are *Introduction to Art History* and *Introduction to Statistics*.

218. Standards should be applied. If they're not, they're not standards.

219. When people tell you, "You're impossible to reach," they're really telling you one of the following things:

- You're slowing down decisions.

- You didn't call me back.

- I need more attention.

- Readjust your schedule, you're killing yourself.

220. Don't get too attached to your office or cube and don't spend a great deal of time decorating it. Chances are good that you'll end up sharing it, anyway.

221. If you tell your boss you have another offer, be prepared to quit.

222. The vast majority of articles written about any organization are accurate. Business journalists don't make things up.

223. Bean-counter jokes about senior management are rarely funny and say nothing more than someone is minding the store.

224. When someone submits their resignation, just accept it. Trying to talk someone out of it will never work, in business as in love.

225. When someone resigns and then changes their mind, start looking for a replacement. It's only a matter of time before they resign again.

226. Breakfast meetings are often very effective because there are fewer distractions. There is not much else to do and people don't feel guilty for what they should have been doing.

227. Make sure you don't leave the bathroom with little paper-towel balls all over your face.

228. When giving a presentation, there is a direct relationship between lighting and sleeping. The darker the room, the more members of the audience who will sleep.

229. When you hear, "With all we've been through together," it means you are about to get to a deeper level of friendship with someone—or get fired.

230. Organizations are often like the emperor with no clothes. Everyone talks about how fine the suit is, but the subjects of the kingdom know there is nothing there.

231. People will see you in your car when you're singing, playing the air guitar, or drumming on the steering wheel. Do it anyway.

232. Careers built on listening are more rewarding than careers built on talking.

233. Don't let people make paper-clip chains at your desk.

234. Don't spend a lot of time telling people what they already know.

235. Know what "extremely urgent" means. Usually, unless there's blood involved, it's not that important.

236. Don't go on *Oprah* or *Geraldo* when they're talking about Bosses from Hell unless you've just won the lottery.

237. Interruptions in meetings are to be avoided, especially if it's your meeting.

238. President George Bush was wrong about the "vision thing." Activity to some end is much more important than retreats and announcements.

239. Never ask someone who stays home with children if they work.

240. If work isn't getting done, reprimands are rarely the answer.

241. Make morale on Monday morning the same as it was on Friday afternoon.

242. Having both standards and flexibility can be done. It's just not easy.

243. Describe your job as if it's the most interesting one in the world—even if it's not.

244. If you leave a meeting talking to yourself, you didn't accomplish what you wanted. Don't call another meeting. Get it done a different way.

245. Stealing stuff from hotels makes your luggage heavier and hotels more expensive.

246. Never take carry-on luggage that's bigger than your car.

247. Assume that you will not be able to find the light switches or thermostats in hotel rooms. Until there is some standardization, which there will never be, assume you will enter stumbling around in the dark in a room that is too hot or too cold.

248. Belching and other bodily noises embarrass everyone around you. Don't do them.

249. Take diversity training seriously.

250. Getting paid for not working serves neither you nor the company. Find something worthwhile to get paid for.

251. Never put anyone on hold for longer than one minute, unless the caller enjoys being left on hold.

252. When someone asks, "Do you have a minute?," know that they're really asking for at least twenty.

253. Keep a bag of candy hidden in your desk for emergencies.

254. When mysterious things show up on your computer screen, it's never a good sign. Call the help desk or the computer dealer. As helpful or unhelpful as they might be, there is no other choice.

255. People who don't smoke often have strong feelings about secondhand smoke.

256. Being too busy with no time to think is the common denominator of work. Adjust the numerator so the equation works for you.

257. Managers more concerned with power and ego than productivity and employees are destined to fail. It just may take a while.

258. The fastest way to solve the problem of too many meetings may be to change the role of middle managers.

259. There is no relationship between jobs being open and having them posted internally. There is always a hidden job market.

260. No one should come to work and have to walk on eggs. It would be better to walk the people creating this environment out the door.

261. If you call in sick, don't expect anyone to believe that you really are ill.

262. V.S.O.P. (Visible Signs of Progress) is often more important than million-dollar strategy reports.

263. Good managers do not automatically back another manager over the truth.

264. Being asked to work more hours while pay levels stay flat or go down is a deadly combination.

265. New company names, logos, and organization charts rarely create change. Change happens when work is altered.

266. Keep a *Rand McNally Road Atlas* at work. It will help you know where you're going, know where other people are, or plan your escape.

267. Learn the basic Internet lingo. A "newbie" is a Net virgin; "flaming" means attacking someone electronically.

268. No amount of pride should get in the way of finding a job to feed your family.

269. Never settle for a job, but be realistic about the kinds of jobs for which you are qualified.

270. Life experience is more important than job experience.

271. Being labeled a part of Generation X is not an excuse for believing there is no future. The opportunities have always been there and always will be. It's only the labels that change.

272. If everyone is making jokes like "Last one out, turn out the lights," make sure you're not last out.

273. You know you've made it when you have a vacation home and time to enjoy it.

274. Fantasies are a great motivator. Just don't get carried away in the implementation plan.

275. Be prepared to be fired if you take anything that remotely resembles a weapon to work.

276. If you think you need a weapon at work—QUIT.

277. A whistle and a clipboard will often put you in charge.

278. Nothing kills morale faster than politics and favoritism.

279. Spend five minutes occasionally just reflecting on what you're spending your time doing and ask yourself if you've become exactly what you thought you never would.

280. There is no greater joy than going home to hear the patter of little feet and voices screaming with glee rushing to meet you.

281. Don't name your children anything that is likely to be confused with the names of dogs or horses.

282. There are no alternatives to practice and experience.

283. Never clip your nails or pick your teeth where you can be seen or heard.

284. There is no reason good enough not to wear comfortable shoes at work.

285. Wearing earphones doesn't give you the license to yell at those who are not.

286. In these days of the Internet and incredible technological breakthroughs, be joyous if you can connect to your office network from a remote location.

287. Three-hundred-sixty-degree reviews can be dangerous. Don't be the first one to review the boss for the record.

288. Don't play saxophone tapes in the office. It reminds everyone of sex.

289. Meaningful work is when you're both committed and engaged.

290. Have a short answer ready for the question, "Where are you from?"

291. Don't answer your phone if you are unable to speak to the caller—like when you have a roomful of people or a mouthful of food.

292. One measure of productivity is not paying for what no one is doing.

293. If your company has had more than two presidents in a year and everyone says it's just a coincidence, start asking lots of questions.

294. Big fires from little fires grow. If there are a bunch of little things wrong that never get fixed, they will eventually kill the company.

295. There is no feeling more relieving than showing up at class when you think you're having a test and spotting a substitute teacher. Remember that when you constantly set unreasonable goals for your team.

296. Never drink alcohol during an interview, even if the interviewer is.

297. Save decorative stationery for personal notes. Kittens and balloons will not help you in the business world.

298. Hire strippers and Rodney Dangerfield impersonators to appear at work only if you place the order in someone else's name.

299. In a sales situation, give the impression that you love what you do.

300. Never get in contests with others about who is working hardest. It's not a contest you want to win.

301. Being direct may catch people off guard, but they almost always appreciate it.

302. In stressful situations, a little humor will tell people you haven't lost touch with reality.

303. When a customer says, "This isn't what I had envisioned," it means, "I don't have what I want."

304. Even though many people don't like National Secretaries Day (except florists), we still have to celebrate it.

305. Know the fire/earthquake escape route from your office.

306. If you absolutely must work on a weekend, do it on Saturday. If you absolutely have to study on a weekend, do it on Sunday.

307. When communication is cited as the big problem, it usually means no one is listening, not no one is talking.

308. Manage the morale, the messages, and the doughnuts. Everything else will fall into place.

309. Use protection. Always have a résumé ready with at least a cool iron close to the fire.

310. When you're starting a new job, ask the stupid questions while you can.

311. Luckily all job candidates believe they can solve the organization's problems as they're revealed during the interview process. Otherwise, no one would ever change jobs.

312. When working out of your home, get up and take a shower or put your makeup on as if you were about to go somewhere. You'll be productive faster.

313. Never baby-sit the children of your boss.

314. Be aware and vigilantly careful when reciting or punching in your phone credit card. Someone could be watching or listening.

315. Never dress up for Halloween as the chairman of the board.

316. The difference between a system bug and a system enhancement is all perception.

317. If you lose one button on a button-down shirt, either get a button and needle and thread or buy a new shirt.

318. Rotating bald tires is a huge activity that changes nothing. It's a good metaphor by which to measure your own activities.

319. People who believe they are empowered will do more than the company expects if they have any idea what the company expects.

320. Progress and improvements are made day-to-day, not year-to-year.

321. If all the office cleaners know your name, you're working too hard.

322. Close to customers is a relative term. If you can't see them or can't talk to them, you're not close.

323. Even sports-and-fitness companies have cookies and ice cream at meetings. Go ahead, indulge.

324. If you work in a consumer product company, expect your circle of family and friends to grow during the holidays.

325. Print E-mail messages only if you need to show the document to someone else. Otherwise, respond or deal with the message.

326. Don't use the letters *i.e.* in speaking.

327. Fight feelings of entitlement. Feeling entitled will not motivate you to perform or help you get what you want and deserve.

328. When someone in the systems group tells you that "You can have it good, fast, or cheap—pick any two," pick two and hold them to it.

329. Managers doing too much clerical work is a sign of a bad job or a bad manager.

330. An internal promotion is one of the most powerful signals the company can send you about your perceived value. If you're continually passed over, that's also a signal.

331. There is no need to pay for suggestions. Employees will gladly provide suggestions if they believe someone will listen and act. Who stands to gain more than the employees?

332. The "permanent record" is a powerful and mystical tool. Don't let it intimidate you.

333. Understanding how pay is administered and how decisions are made could save some heartache at raise time.

334. Trying to separate performance reviews from pay decisions is like taking the jelly out of the doughnut.

335. There are plenty of other ways to cut costs besides cutting pay.

336. A college degree cannot substitute for experience, but it can help you get ready. Make sure you get experience.

337. Structure is necessary but bureaucracy is not. Don't confuse them.

338. Don't spend a lot of time "witch hunting." In the end, it doesn't matter who did it. Who fixed it matters.

339. People want to work safely. No one needs incentives, just reminders.

340. Never trust hotel clock-radio alarms. Never believe you will be able to figure out a hotel clock-radio.

341. There is a direct relationship: The more time you spend decorating your office or cube, the more you will be moved.

342. On the Friday afternoon preceding a three-day weekend, expect to be the only one working.

343. Know the difference between wine categories. "Red" and "white" are not enough.

344. If you're entitled to overtime pay, claim it. If you're gaming the system, don't claim it. Someone will catch on.

345. Treatment of employees, morale, leadership, and quality are so interrelated that one cannot change without affecting the others. Know which ones you can make better.

346. Empowerment means you can sign off on something. Don't get mad, deal with it.

347. Read *USA Today* for trends, the *New York Times* for depth, and the comic strip "Dilbert" for the truth.

348. When faced with difficult decisions or tight deadlines, ask yourself, "What's the worst that can happen if . . . ?" The answer is usually not as bad as you feared.

349. Stacking pink telephone-message slips proudly means you're talking on the phone too much to get anything real done or that you don't return calls. Neither habit is advisable.

350. Optimism will get you farther at work than obnoxiousness.

351. Never take calculus, chemistry, and accounting in the same semester. Never assume projects at work that will remind you of the time you took those three classes at the same time.

352. Create combinations of what you want to do and where you want to live. Play with the combinations as the options roll in.

353. Making grocery lists during staff meetings is in bad form. It will also make you hungry.

354. Wordsmithing is never done well in a committee.

355. No standards + no measures + no penalties = no direction

356. Nothing discloses more about what you think is important than your schedule.

357. De facto means no one ever made the decision but now we're stuck with it. Revisit those decisions.

358. "If you want to make enemies, try to change something."
—President Woodrow Wilson

359. Checking phone mail from the road more frequently than once every fifteen minutes is a sickness.

360. Tweaking organizations will create a lot of tweaks but no real change.

361. If you think you'll need a rental car, you probably will. Taxis are only an efficient travel mode in big cities. The bigger the city, the more efficient.

362. If you're meeting someone for the first time in a social spot, know how to describe yourself in a nonself-aggrandizing way. "I'll be easy to spot, I look like Michelle Pfeiffer" is not a good descriptor.

363. Never ask someone if you can pick their brains. You're not dealing with chicken bones.

364. Never get drunk with someone who can fire you.

365. Accidental meetings, in the halls or at the coffee wagon, can be more valuable than formal meetings. Circulate.

366. If you don't go to church, believe in something.

367. Give money to street performers that you enjoy.

368. Wait until you see your co-workers before you buy your entire wardrobe.

369. On average, we all only live for about 25,000 days. Take out the calculator, plot where you are, and don't dwell on what you've missed. Just enjoy the rest. Not through work alone, but through everything that is life.

Epilogue

Readers, friends, co-workers, airline-seat partners, casual observers, and any number of surprising sources continue to bring ideas to my attention. Keep those cards and letters coming! As the workplace changes, so do the rules. And those new rules need to be broadcast. These books seem to be a good forum. If you have a pearl of wisdom to contribute, send it to the address below, and if it is used, you will receive full acknowledgment in future books.

Richard A. Moran
P. O. Box 29134
San Francisco, CA 94129-0134

Contributors

The following individuals and groups generated ideas, made suggestions, and wrote in with aphorisms that were considered or used:

Hi Tech Public Relations

Delta Upsilon Fraternity

Wilford A. Butler

Matthew Shinkman

Deborah Zaslov

J. David Martin

John R. Day
Hugh Van Dusen
Jeff Whitton
William J. Powers, Jr.
Kristy Howard-Clark